THE INSIDE SECRETS TO
BUILDING AND TIMBER PEST INSPECTIONS

AN INSPECTOR'S GUIDE TO CHOOSING YOUR NEW HOME

STUART G MARSAY BSC MRICS

First published by Ultimate World Publishing 2020
Copyright © Stuart G Marsay

ISBN

Paperback – 978-1-922372-34-5
Ebook – 978-1-922372-35-2

Stuart G Marsay has asserted his right under the Copyright, Designs and Patents Act 1988 to be identified as the author of this work. The information in this book is based on the author's experiences and opinions. The publisher specifically disclaims responsibility for any adverse consequences, which may result from use of the information contained herein. Permission to use information has been sought by the author. Any breaches will be rectified in further editions of the book.

All rights reserved. No part of this publication may be reproduced, stored in or introduced into a retrieval system, or transmitted in any form, or by any means (electronic, mechanical, photocopying, recording or otherwise) without the prior written permission of the author. Any person who does any unauthorised act in relation to this publication may be liable to criminal prosecution and civil claims for damages. Enquiries should be made through the publisher.

Cover design: Ultimate World Publishing
Layout and typesetting: Ultimate World Publishing
Editor: Hayley Ward
Cover images: rawmn–Shutterstock.com (Background Modern House) GraphicsRF–Shutterstock.com (Cartoon Wooden House) Refluo–Shutterstock.com (Cartoon Termite)

Ultimate World Publishing
Diamond Creek,
Victoria Australia 3089
www.writeabook.com.au

CONTENTS

Preface v
Part 1: Getting Started 1
Part 2: External 7
    Residential foundations 9
    External walls 19
    Windows 29
    External doors 39
    Roof 43
    Water systems 59
    Garden and landscaping 67
Part 3: Internal 85
    Walls 87
    Finishes – internal wall and ceilings 89
    Floors 93
    Fans and air conditioning 95
    Doors 97
    Internal timberwork 101
    Internal plumbing 113
    Termite damage 117
Where to next? 123

PREFACE

Stuart has been part of the building and property industry for all of his working life; some 36 years to date. Stuart started his career in 1981 as an apprentice carpenter and joiner, which he considers to be a noble trade. Stuart served his four-year apprenticeship in a small local building company, learning his craft across all joinery disciplines. Stuart worked his way up to Foreman Joiner and General Site Foreman, responsible for all site trades, and ultimately becoming a Building Site Manager. Stuart's keenness and craving for knowledge within the building industry took him all around the UK and to North Africa (Algeria).

Upon meeting his future wife Vicky, they moved a short distance from the seaside town of Scarborough in the UK and made a home in the beautiful, historic city of York. Stuart returned to higher education to obtain his Higher National Certificate in Building Studies, studying for three years at York Technical College (Australian TAFE equivalent) and a further three years to achieve a BSc in Building Surveying from Sheffield Hallam University.

In an industry where experience really counts, Stuart is a member of the Royal Institution of Chartered Surveyors in two disciplines: Property Valuation and Building Surveying/Building Pathology.

While studying, Stuart worked for a newly-formed local social housing association as a Building Inspector, and eventually Building Surveyor, responsible for the maintenance and upkeep of their large housing stock. Millions of pounds were spent each year on capital repair/improvement works on thousands of homes. It was a very busy and exciting time, as every conceivable type of repair/refurbishment work was undertaken to the property portfolio.

After seven years with the housing association, Stuart moved to a large retail company as the Contracts and Maintenance Manager, responsible for the maintenance and upkeep of over 250 retail stores across the UK. His responsibilities included the day-to-day management of the retail stores' maintenance issues, managing a team of property professionals.

The business was also in an expansion phase of its existence, with 30 new stores and 35 refurbishments a year, which Stuart project-managed.

Not content with his current success, Stuart was headhunted to take a position with an internationally-recognised multidiscipline surveying practice, as a Senior Building Surveyor. Stuart provided services to motor trade companies concerning the

PREFACE

acquisition of land and subsequent project management of new car and truck sales, service and body shop developments, for many of the internationally-recognised high street dealerships across the UK.

An opportunity arose for Stuart to run the Building Surveying and Valuation department of a small residential real estate and valuation company. Providing services to all the main street banks and private clients, Stuart was instrumental in building the Property Valuation and Survey department and after many years, left the company as a full equity Director. The company continues to be a multi-award-winning private enterprise.

Over the years, Stuart has guided thousands of residential buyers through the acquisition and disposal of properties, at all times striving to deliver service and results well beyond his client's expectations.

From 2010 to 2017, Stuart held the position of Course Coordinator and Lecturer in Property Economics and Development at the University of the Sunshine Coast, writing and lecturing in PED 110 and PED121 – Residential and Commercial Building Studies.

Stuart enjoys his free time with his competitive, sporting-mad family, his wife Vicky, and his five children, who are all actively involved in community sporting events.

Working as a Property Inspector in Australia undertaking pre-purchase Building and Timber Pest Inspections for clients from all walks of life, Stuart realised that unless employed in the building trade, his clients had little to no experience of evaluating a property they were potentially committing to purchase. He recognised that although purchasers pay for the services of a local inspector to check the property before they go contractually unconditional, it would be beneficial for both sellers and purchasers to refer to an easy to read and follow book of handy hints and pointers, simply illustrated, to help sellers prepare for a home to take to market, or for purchasers to be better informed on what to look for when viewing a potential new home.

It should be stressed at this point that it takes years of training and nationally-recognised qualifications to act on a client's behalf, however, would it not make sense to have an idea of what the professional inspectors are looking for?

As such, Stuart has put together this helpful compendium for both buyers and sellers, in the hope that post reading this book, you will never look at a property in the same way again.

PART 1

Getting Started

Check out the property in advance

Look at the property prior to attending an open home or viewing by appointment. Visit the street at a time when there may be activity, a time when everyone is at home, for example, post-school time, on a weeknight.

When arriving at the property you are interested in viewing, drive up and down the street, paying particular attention to the type of properties that make up the street; type and age, likely living accommodation and age group/demographics of the occupants. This will give you an idea of who your neighbours may be. For example, a street full of noisy children might not appeal to a retiree couple but be ideal for expecting parents or a young family. Also, pay attention to the condition of the neighbours' gardens — are they tidy and well-tended? Are there car parts or a part completed hobby restoration on the nature strip?

Most inspectors always follow a set pattern or MO (Modus Operandi) when viewing a property; this ensures that they follow the same routine of information-gathering at each property they visit.

View the property from the front elevation, i.e. with your back to the street; take your time and take in everything in view. Assess the house yard and take a stroll around the yard in a clockwise manner; front, left, rear and right-hand yards around the property. Take your time and take in what you see. Don't worry about missing anything, the idea of this first time walk around is to get your subconscious mind to pay attention and to clear your mind of the daily junk that rattles around in there; for example, what's for tea, don't forget to pick up the kids, the car needs fuel, etc. This process will give you your first opinion of the place. Is it tidy and well presented? There are usually tell-tale signs as to the type of people who live in the house, as most but not all occupants try to hide this, through fastidious tidying up prior to the open home.

How to record your findings

A building inspector will have his or her own way of recording the building information taken during an inspection. This should follow a set method and either use a tablet (iPad or Samsung device) or traditional paper note method (field sheets). I prefer to use a pencil and paper note format, with a set of pre-existing questions and tick boxes. Standard note-taking ensures that each inspection is undertaken to the same standard and building elements are not missed or overlooked due to distractions, possibly from the Real Estate Agent or purchaser asking questions during the inspection. I also turn off my mobile phone during the inspection to reduce possible distractions. Think of it as an exam situation, and why wouldn't you? You have just embarked on a journey which may culminate in the largest purchase of your life.

After many years of inspecting/surveying buildings, note collation becomes an aide memoir rather than a prompt. The report is then written post-inspection— with the use of the information gathered and noted on the field sheets, and photographs. I tend to take heaps of photographs, even if I have no intention of using them in the report. Cleverly taken photographs of a walk around the property is a fantastic way of preparing for the written report, with modern cameras/mobiles also able to take video footage. I'm not suggesting potential purchasers walk around filming the property, as this may be seen as an infringement of the vendor's privacy. This is best left to the inspector!

Tools of the trade

When inspecting a property, the Building and Pest Inspector will use the following tools:

- **Donger** – a tapping device which is a stick not dissimilar to a golf club shaft with a ball on the end. This is used to tap or sound out the timber finishes on the inside and outside of the house; for example, skirting boards, window frames, architraves, fascia and soffit boarding, timber cover strips and the like. The inspector is looking for an audible high pitch tapping noise, which is the sound that timber in good condition makes. A low pitch dull sound indicates that the timber is in poor order, and further investigation is advised to determine the extent of any defective areas.

- **Moisture meter** – there are a number of meters available on the market, with the favoured meter being Tramex, a tool that is well-respected in the property inspection industry.

- New technologies are also available, including **Termatrac T3I**, which is a device that can detect termite activity and moisture within the walls of a property.

- **Thermal imaging cameras** – Flir is a recognised market leader and respected in the industry. It is a valuable tool when used in conjunction with the above.

- **Binoculars, ladders, magnifying glass, torch, and screwdriver** for prodding timberwork.

- **Protective clothing** – overalls, protective hat, mask, gloves, and firm footwear.

Below is a photograph of the equipment listed above

The greatest tool an inspector has is their knowledge. It is always important to ascertain the experience of the professional you are considering employing to undertake the important task of assessing your property. An individual who has extensive knowledge of building types and methods, but more importantly building defects, their detection, and is able to convey that information to you in a balanced, supportive and thoughtful way, is key and a priceless asset.

Although the professional's price/fee is important, it is also critical to ensure they are up to the task.

PART 2
EXTERNAL

RESIDENTIAL FOUNDATIONS

The following illustrations depict the more popular methods of residential foundation construction.

Infill concrete slabs

Infill concrete slabs consist of the external walls of a property being constructed off a strip foundation, which is formed within a trench beneath the ground. The depth and design of the footing is calculated and provided by a structural engineer, the external wall of the property is then constructed upon it, and as it reaches the proposed ground floor level a concrete slab is poured across the footprint of the site, up to the inner side of the external brick wall. This type of construction has become less popular and although perfectly acceptable, can be prone to allowing hidden termite access to the property.

Termites can gain access to the timber frame and internal timbers by travelling unseen up the rear of the brick wall between wall and infill floor slab. Suitable termite management is essential.

The photograph shows the usual detail of an infill slab construction. With this design, you will not see the concrete edge of the floor slab, because this is hidden behind the brick or blockwork. The load from the wall and house is borne upon the foundation strip, which is beneath the ground.

Concrete slab on ground

Slab on ground, as this type of foundation support is commonly known, consists of a substantial concrete raft laid on the dirt and is designed by a structural engineer to provide support to the proposed house that will sit upon it. The foundation acts as a raft, floating or sitting directly on top of the ground.

This type of foundation is usually covered by floor coverings, for example, ceramic tiles, carpet, laminated floor coverings and the like. Indicators of defects in the slab may manifest as a tear in the tile coverings, which would look like a crack running through the tile floor, width or lengthways of a room or hallway.

The best place to examine a concrete slab surface is within the garage, as the floor finish is usually the natural concrete. Look for cracks within the top of the floor. Fine hairline cracks may be due to the concrete slab drying out a little too quickly, because of climatic conditions. Warm dry weather and wind can lead to surface shrinkage cracking. Should cracks be apparent and visible, make a note and request the inspector to take a look. He can then advise if there is any cause for concern or if it's just superficial and restricted to the surface.

Concrete raft foundation prior to construction of the house superstructure.

The pipes passing through the slab are service pipes for bathroom and kitchen/laundry.

Stumps - timber or concrete

A traditional foundation method generally employed to support timber–framed Queenslander style homes, although not restricted to them. The defects to look for are as follows:

- Fungal decay within timber stumps. There are two main stages of decay:
    1) Decaying timber
    2) Decayed timber.

When timber comes into contact or is part buried into the ground, it is not a matter of if, but when, fungal decay or timber pest attack will occur. Admittedly, timber preservatives will, if applied properly, reduce the onset of decay and pest attack, but eventually they will succumb; it's the natural order of things. So, how do we identify timber fungal and pest attack?

Look for the following:

- Soft, spongy external face of the timber, which will allow you to push your finger into and beyond the outer surface.
- Cuboidal cracking — this is where the timber splits into small square blocks, and at this stage has lost its strength.
- The presence of carpenter ants within the body of the timber — they like to inhabit decaying timber.
- Fruiting bodies — this is where the fungus matures and creates sacks or mushroom-like growths full of spores, and if disturbed, they pop and release millions of new spores into the air.

Block wall.

Timber in contact with the ground, conducive for termite activity, and fungal decay.

Timber stump with fungal decay, where it meets the ground. The stump is now unable to carry the load it was intended for. The darker shading is fungal decay within the timber.

Timber stump with decay to the base.

This stump is not in contact with the structure above, therefore not offering any structural support.

This stump looked in a serviceable condition above ground level but was easily pushed over to reveal extensive fungal decay. On this particular property, a high percentage were in various stages of decomposition with fungal decay and termite workings.

This is an example of a timber stump that appeared to be in a serviceable condition above ground, but further investigation revealed the stump was completely decayed just 50mm beneath what was visible.

Pole supports - timber or steel

This method is used on a sloping site, with either timber or steel support framework. Some surfaces of the posts and framework will be above eye height. It is a little more difficult to visually detect all failures, but generally what you should look for is fungal fruiting bodies on the surface of the timber, any dark patches which may indicate fungal decay, holes, splits and depressions within the timber surfaces, especially at junctures, joints and along the top and outer edges of timbers which are exposed to the weather.

There are a number of different types of fungus that destroy timber. Each fungus has its own unique features, but ultimately they all lead to the decomposition of the timber they are attacking. Wet rot is usually restricted to a particular area of timber which it is breaking down. Even if sporadically in evidence around the external timbers of a property, wet rot can still be costly to effect remedial repair works. Access is a cost consideration, for example, a sloping /steep block or two or more storey property may require scaffolding for safe working access.

Corrosion of the steel fixing bolts will generally be evident by brown or orange staining around and below fixings — this is oxidisation of ferrous metals. Some lower quality stainless steel will also succumb to the elements, certainly the closer to the beach you are. Steel support frames are usually electroplated ferrous metal, which has a decorative paint coating to protect it from the elements. In cases where suitable maintenance has not been maintained or the building environment allows for pooling/standing water at the base of the poles, corrosion can take place.

When inspecting a pole house, always pay attention to the surface condition of the support framework – has it been well maintained, is there any sign of corrosion on any of the surfaces, junctures or where the frame has been jointed? Is there any corrosion at the base of the pole where it meets the ground? Is there any evidence of standing water around the framework bases? Even in a dry period, you can usually see a depression around the base of the pole where water may stand; this linked to a ring of corrosion around the base would indicate there might be a problem. If the corrosion is minor and on the surface, preparation removal of the surface rust corrosion and redecoration will usually be adequate. Standing water can be rectified by re-grading the ground around the affected area and in some cases installation of land drainage to re-divert the standing water.

In this photograph there is evidence of corrosion to the bottom of a steel post support, if left unattended will corrode fully this is compromising its load bearing capacity.

Brick, concrete block, or solid concrete

It is generally easy to note if there are any obvious defects concerning brick or blockwork stump walls, for example:

- Are they in vertical alignment and in contact with the steel or timber frame above, i.e. carrying weight?
- Can you see any deflection of the beam/joist from stump to stump? This may indicate settlement/downward movement of a stump or the stumps may be too wide apart if deflection/sagging of the floor joist is evident.
- Has the stump got a termite/ant cap on the top, and is it in good order, with no signs of corrosion?

Solid concrete piers should visually be free from significant cracks. If you note cracking and loss of the outer concrete face of the stump, this may be due to the way they were installed, or carbonation of concrete may be taking place. In simple terms, the chemical PH of the concrete has altered through a chemical reaction between carbon dioxide in the air, which penetrates the concrete pores and reacts with calcium hydroxide. This reduces the concrete's natural alkalinity, corrosion can then affect the concrete reinforcement, which as it corrodes, expands and blows off the eternal concrete protection, exposing the steel to the elements. This process accelerates decomposition and reduces the strength of the concrete. Reduced strength of the pier naturally affects the stability of the building above.

RESIDENTIAL FOUNDATIONS

Concrete block stump with ant cap on the top. The stump is supporting part of the weight of the house above.

This is an example of how not to replace a timber stump with a concrete one. This will be the likely cause of uneven floor finishes and problems with doors and cabinets not operating properly. This stump would need to be removed and replaced by a competent licensed builder.

Concrete stump with ant cap on the top. You should also check for the existence of steel tie-downs; a steel bracket that is fixed to both the upper portion of the concrete stump and the timber structure above (cyclone resistance).

The ant cap is corroded out. If there is unseen corrosion, the cap would be compromised and may allow the passage of termites into the main building structure, should termites be active in the stump.

EXTERNAL WALLS

There are a number of different configurations regarding residential dwellings, and not all houses are consistent in build, i.e. can be made up of different types of materials. In the eyes of the architect, the use of different building materials gives the property artistic/architectural merit. The use of different materials will mean that the external façade of the building will age at different rates/speeds, with the lightweight elements succumbing, being affected by the climate more readily than say brick or blockwork. Geographical location and orientation is also a factor affecting the serviceability of a building product, and its proximity to the harsh elements of the sea. Coastal against inland property bring their own set of design difficulties for the architect. That being said, modern weatherboarding and sheet cladding offers the opportunity for the developer to create more architecturally-appealing homes. To potential purchasers, a balancing act of functionality over cost and form is required.

The following illustrations depict the more popular methods of external wall construction, and visual defects you may encounter:

- Full brick walls are solid 225mm thick with no cavity between the inner and outer face of the wall.

- Types of failure may manifest in the form of stepped cracking within the brick work, which may indicate settlement of the foundations. Depending on the width, length and age of the crack, will allow the inspector to determine if the movement is recent and ongoing, or historical and stable. The inspector may suggest further investigation by a structural engineer or licensed builder in some cases.

- Older brick properties may also have vertical cracking that follows the window or door opening, part way along the length of a wall. This may be due to expansion and contraction of the brickwork along the length of the wall. Modern properties incorporate vertical expansion joints at predetermined locations, to allow for natural movement, expansion and contraction of the building materials.

EXTERNAL WALLS

Vertical crack/tear within the external face of the brickwork. The crack is even for the full length, which indicates it is most likely a thermal expansion crack. Your inspector would be able to advise on any course of action.

Vertical crack within a concrete block wall beneath a property. This is a load-bearing wall. There is also additional cracking within adjacent walls. Further investigation is required here to determine the cause and type of remedial action required.

Stepped cracking visible within the external brick wall. The crack also runs along the window frame vertically to the ground. This will depict foundation movement. Take note of the immediate surroundings for trees and large bushes or shrubs, as feeder roots can cause significant foundation problems. This type of failure will require the advice from a licensed structural engineer.

Cladding or weatherboarding with timber frame

Timber frames with cement-based cladding or plywood, although very serviceable, brings its own serviceability issues. Brittle cement-based products don't stand up to impact damage and are not always easy to effect repairs, without it being noticeable. It usually involves full removal of the affected panel and subsequent reinstatement, so it's important to be aware that a small area of damaged boarding may be more costly than first envisaged.

Where timber sheeting is employed as external cladding, pay attention to joints and junctures, as any deterioration of the decorative waterproof covering can lead to decay taking hold, which will not always be visible until complete decomposition has started to take place and failure of the product has commenced. The illustration below shows decomposition of a cladding product. Note that the repair will also involve redecoration; do you think you will be able to adequately match the paint finish with years of weather and sunlight, UV degradation?

EXTERNAL WALLS

Fungal decay within the plywood cladding of the external wall, visible because water has penetrated the junction between two boards. It is always prudent when viewing the external façade to pay attention to junctions and joints where there is a natural weak point; decay will be more visible at these locations.

Brick veneer and timber framed

This is a two-storey property under construction. The timber frame is exposed with the blue sheeting visible (moisture barrier). The green material at the bottom is the termite management system running around the perimeter of the building. The bricks in the foreground will be laid to create the external wall of the property, which is either left as a brick finish or in this case, render finished. All the load of the structure is borne by the timber frame and not the brickwork, which is there to provide weatherproofing.

Blockwork with a cement coating

External concrete block wall with a cement covering known as bagging.

This is a traditional method of finishing either brick or block walls and can help with establishing the age of a dwelling.

Blockwork and render

Concrete block wall, hollow core blocks filled with concrete.

Example of a hollow core concrete block (Besser blocks) before it is walled. These are generally filled with concrete once in place.

EXTERNAL WALLS

Asbestos sheet material

This material is extremely weather and environmentally durable. However, it does not react well to impact damage. External boarding may be painted or left in its naked grey state. Board junction joints are usually covered with a timber cover strip to assist in excluding rainwater.

As you walk around the property, look for cover strips which correspond to the joints of the boarding. Homes pre-2003 may have asbestos products within some building products; your building inspector will be able to determine if an asbestos audit is required.

Impact damage to an asbestos sheet; the cover strip is also deformed.

External façade asbestos sheeting with joint cover strip. Modern architecturally-designed houses also use cover strips to cover joints to boarding. Establishing the age of the building will allow the building inspector to determine if further investigation is warranted, to determine the type of sheeting material used.

Damp penetration

Damp isn't restricted to roof penetration; in older properties it can also manifest from rising damp, coming up from the subfloor. This can usually be seen as a tide mark. With damp penetration comes efflorescence — this is the deposit of natural salts from within the building products — bricks, blocks and cement — that are deposited on the surface when water migration stops, and evaporation takes place.

Water penetration through a block wall leaving efflorescence (salts on the surface of the block wall).

EXTERNAL WALLS

Water markings on the inner side of a lower ground wall. This is a clear indication that water penetration has or is taking place. Further investigation is required if damp is evident, as repair may be costly.

WINDOWS

Window frames usually employ a timber reveal or lining on the inside of the window, to seal the juncture between the frame and plasterboard wall. This timber, like any other softwood, is prone to fungal decay. The usual failing of the timber is due to condensation forming on the window glazing; water runs down the glass and collects on the window reveal/sill. Although the timber is usually painted and sealed, the ends or edges of the timber where it abuts the window frame have, at best, usually only received a primer coat of paint before installation and will be susceptible to moisture penetration. Fungal spores are naturally found floating around in the atmosphere. These spores are very opportunistic and will propagate where the moisture levels/humidity is stable. Rot therefore takes hold in the timber edge or where jointed. Because timber is a natural product, it moves — twisting, expanding and contracting — following its local microclimate. This creates failures in the paint covering and allows moisture to penetrate. Once rot/fungal decay takes hold, the timber will continue to decompose until it becomes fully decayed and failure takes place.

Older properties with timber windows are susceptible to the windows becoming weathered, and over time, they will become ill-fitting, and will, if the weather conditions are correct, allow water penetration. You can usually notice water markings or pattern staining on the inner surfaces around windows that are not fully weather tight. Timber windows are also susceptible to twist and swelling, due to absorption of moisture, which may make them difficult to operate and close to latch.

The following illustrations depict the more popular window details and visual defects you may come across. Please note, 'sash' is the name for the opening part of the window frame.

Aluminium horizontal sliding sash

- Neoprene seals (black rubber material between the glass and frame) suffer from UV degradation and become hard and fall apart/shrink. A simple visual inspection will determine the condition of this part of the window frame. The frame should be smooth and no evidence of shrinkage at mitre, (corner) junctions.

- The wheels on the bottom of the larger, heavier sliding sashes become worn and make opening and closing the window difficult. The larger the sash, the more it will weigh, therefore the more difficult it will be to operate over time, as the wheels become worn.

- Smaller sliding sashes infrequently are ill-fitting within the window frame and may suffer from a rocking motion when the operator is sliding the sash open and closed. The window is still functional, however, to some it will be a source of frustration, as it is a little difficult to operate, but nevertheless still functional overall (toilet windows are the usual culprit for this minor defect).

- It is common practice for modern aluminium/metal windows to employ a plastic latch locking mechanism. The lower cost market windows don't always have a physical key locking system and just rely on the plastic latch to provide security. Although perfectly adequate when new, in time, they tend to become a little problematic and don't always latch correctly, which creates a security issue. They can appear to be latched but if a gentle force is applied on the sash, they may fail, allowing the window to be opened from outside.

- Saltwater degradation of the frame and welded joints occurs when aluminium windows are close to salt air (beach). Older windows corrode over time, with white bubbling at the mitre joints and around rivets. Most doors and windows remain serviceable, but unfortunately look unsightly.

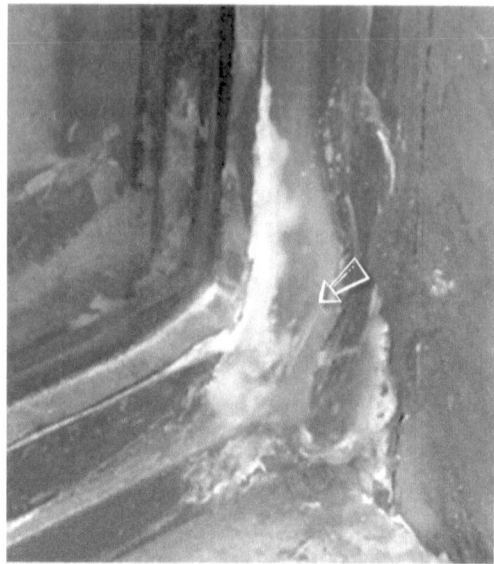

Bottom corner of an aluminium window frame with corrosion taking place.

Aluminium vertical sliding

- Modern vertical sliding sash windows employ a spring mechanism located within the frame. This acts as a balance for the weight of the sash including the glass, thus when you open the sash, it should remain in the position you opened it, whether that's 50mm or fully open. Unfortunately, over time and dependant of factors such as quality of the window frame and proximity to the coast and salt air weather conditions, the spring mechanism begins to fail, and the sash window will not hold its position. In most failure cases, the sash will slowly slide back to the closed position; some may crash down to the closed position.

- Saltwater degradation of the frame and welded joints. White bubbling of the frame (looks like a build-up of salt deposits) leading to loss of paint coverage on the surface of the frame and joints at the frame corners.

The balance springs have failed on the vertically sliding top sash of this bathroom window. These are springs located within the window frame, to counterbalance the weight of the frame and glass, which makes operation of the window quite easy.

Without the balance springs, the sashes are difficult to operate and if you can manage to lift it closed and get it latched, when you open it again, it will slide down into the fully open position. This type of failure of sash balance springs is quite common with older houses and should be anticipated and budgeted for. The condition of the springs will determine if the sash will remain in the position you open it to or will gradually slide or crash fully to the open/closed position, depending if the sash is a top or bottom opening part of the window.

Timber horizontal sliding windows

Less popular in modern times, paint and varnish finished windows suffer from UV degradation, sunlight damage; therefore—higher maintenance costs should be expected to keep the timber in good working order. You may also experience fungal decay within the timber frame because of failure of the protective decorative coating. Most timber frames consist of a hardwood sill with softwood mainframe. It is also not uncommon for a full hardwood or softwood frame – only a trained eye would be able to establish this, I'm afraid.

- Fungal decay within timber framework can take the following forms – darkening and softening of the decorative finishes.

- A spongy feel to timber, which may be along its length or at frame joints.

- The varnish may have cracked and flaked away from the frame, but in some cases paint coverage remains with fungal decay, wood rot has taken hold beyond, out of sight. Decay usually manifests itself in uneven paint finishes, with rutting/grooves in the paint due to lack of structure behind. Subsequent stretching and deterioration of the paint veneer then takes place.

Timber vertical sliding windows

As with the aluminium windows discussed earlier, modern sliding sash windows are balanced by spring mechanisms within the window frame. Naturally there is more weight in a timber frame, opposed to aluminium, therefore, the mechanism needs to be of a suitable strength and quality to remain in service over the life of the window. Additional issues associated with correct function of the sliding window is subsequent paint applications, post installation. Most properties receive external redecoration every five to seven years. If the paint is inappropriately applied to the frame and becomes attached to the sash, the windows will not work correctly. Because timber is a natural product, during heavy rain or if the decorative coating is not kept in a serviceable condition, during inclement weather, the timber will absorb moisture swell and may not operate correctly. It is therefore important to keep up with planned maintenance.

A point to note is that the windows on some of the older Queenslander properties don't employ balancing/counterweights to balance the opening sash. Instead they use a number of metal hooks to allow the window to remain in the open position. Wear and tear to the locking latches can occur over time with older properties, with latches working loose and becoming difficult to operate. Sloppy painting can also affect the use of the latch mechanism.

Traditional vertically sliding sash window within a 100-year-old house. It is important that the sashes are free to operate and not painted shut. Some but not all of the older windows have balance weights within the frame and those that don't have little metal hooks placed at intervals vertically, to support the sash, and stop it crashing closed. You may expect to see two on a sash this size. Another important note is because of the loose fitting of the sash, to ensure it runs freely, the window may rattle in stormy weather and also be draughty.

The window fastener has come loose on this vertically sliding sash window. This is a typical giveaway that the sash doesn't operate freely and is difficult to lock. It's always worthwhile taking a look at the condition of the property window's ironmongery, because if there are a lot of windows servicing the house, it has the potential to get quite expensive if overhaul is necessary, which could eat into your budget.

Timber hinged windows

With older windows, hinges can be rendered almost inoperable by a build-up of paint. Corrosion of the pin of the hinge can also affect functionality. Sprained hinges can make the sash bind, which is where the clapping/closing edge of the sash catches on the frame, or the sash may resist being closed to latch, springing open when you release it.

Natural shrinkage of timber windows, whether old or modern, may also lead to the glass rattling within the frame. This in turn may lead to breakages when operating the window.

Timber hinged (side hung) sash windows.

It is always worth requesting the inspector pay particular attention to the condition of the sashes, to see if there are any tell-tale signs of any possible problems with operation and discuss this at the end of the inspection.

Timber louvre windows

A great creator of airflow through a property, the general rule of thumb for maintenance is the same as timber windows.

Hardwood frame with glass louvres.

EXTERNAL DOORS

External hardwood, softwood and aluminium doors, including bi-fold doors

It is quite easy to recognise a hardwood door on a modern property; they generally have a top and bottom pin hinge that allows the door to open fully with a clear space between the door and frame. These doors are predominantly varnished but can be painted. Most modern designed houses' main entrance doors are protected from the elements/weather by some kind of entrance canopy.

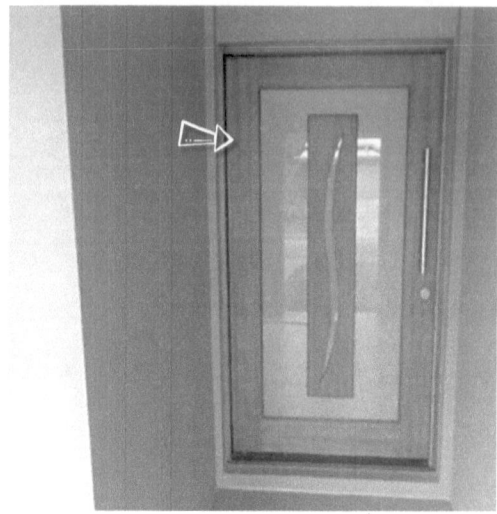

Typical example of a modern hardwood residential front door.

On older properties, the doors may be of a lightweight construction which is either hardboard or plywood with a cardboard (egg box structural element within). These doors are very easy to damage, through impact damage, and can be affected by water/weather damage if in an exposed location, so it is always prudent to pay particular attention to the condition of external entrance doors, as they also obviously provide security to the property. Ironmongery (door furniture) locks and latches on older properties are also problematic and may be prone to being faulty. They can also suffer from delamination; loss of the outer layers of the door. Older lightweight doors are also prone to letting in rainwater at the juncture with the doorframe and threshold in stormy weather, which isn't always visible if a prolonged dry period precedes your viewing of the house. A good tip is to look for water marking pattern stains in the inner side of the door frame or on the floor finishes. This will be discussed later in water and damp penetration.

Bi-fold doors are usually associated with decks, patio or verandas and can be aluminium or timber construction. Problems arise when the doors start to age and suffer from wear and tear, leading to poor operation when opening and closing. It is always worthwhile asking the agent to open and close the doors whilst you are viewing the property. Your inspector will also take a look. Heavy doors are more susceptible to failure of the door track and hinge.

Flyscreens

Always check that the flyscreens are large enough for the window frame that they are employed; in some instances, they are too small or are just generally ill-fitting screens, which are not fit for purpose.

Flyscreen too small for the window opening.

You will most likely come across holes and damaged sections of mesh, normal wear and tear. You will need to undertake repairs, so budget accordingly.

Typical damage caused to flyscreens to watch out for; small holes and tears.

Tear within the flyscreen.

Security screens

These are more substantial than flyscreens and are designed to make it more difficult for an intruder to gain access to the property. There are many products on the market offering various levels of security and quality. It's always worth asking the vendor if they have any technical information available about the manufacturer of the screens. With older properties it is less likely to be forthcoming than a modern property, but always worth a try.

ROOF

Roof coverings

There are a number of materials used to create the water and weather covering on a residential property. Here we examine the most common that you are likely to come across when searching for a new home.

Colorbond Steel

This is a corrugated, very durable sheet−roofing product, which according to the manufacturer has 50 years life expectancy, and comes in an array of colours, designed for Australian weather conditions. A common failure of this type of sheet roofing is the corrosion of the screw fixings, especially if the property is close to the coast. Replacement of the screw fixings is labour−intensive and can prove costly; it is worth noting if there is any visible corrosion to screw heads. Deterioration of the paint covering, UV damage, over time will lead to discolouration/degradation of the paint covering. This is a sign that either redecoration or replacement costs should be budgeted for.

Concrete tile

A very durable roof covering, resistant to salt and frost, and generally considered to be low maintenance, with a reputed 50-year life span, dependent on climatic conditions. These tiles don't, however, like to be walked upon, and can be damaged through impact damage or foot traffic borne upon them. You should therefore seek professional advice if access over the roof coverings is required, to avoid any unwanted repair bills. Concrete tiles come in many colours, and when aged can look dull and detract from the appeal of the property. It is possible, through specialist contractors, to repaint the roof tiles, to give the property a more modern look. This is an option to consider when viewing a property for purchase.

Asbestos

Corrugated sheet material mainly found on older properties, usually working in tandem with asbestos gutters and rainwater pipes. Usually only found on old Queenslanders and fibro houses, and although in many cases the sheeting remains functional and generally weather and watertight, It is best considered obsolete and any prudent purchaser would take into consideration the costs of removal, disposal and upgrading of these materials, because all works undertaken to asbestos are code assessable and will have a premium cost above non—asbestos materials. If in doubt, commission an asbestos audit on the property, to assess the risk of asbestos materials being present.

Galvanised and Galvalume zinc coating roofing.

This corrugated sheet roofing has the more traditional tin roof look that we generally associate with residential roofing, pre introduction to Colorbond.

This type of roofing is prone to corrosion, which is visible as a brown staining on the sheet. This generally leads to pin holes forming at the onset of corrosion and later to full failure and holes within the roof covering. Corrosion also appears along the outer edges of the sheeting above gutters and gable (side walls) of the property, where the edges of the tin sheet is most vulnerable and exposed to the elements, and where the zinc coating may be compromised, due to physical damage during transportation and installation.

Corroded steel roof.

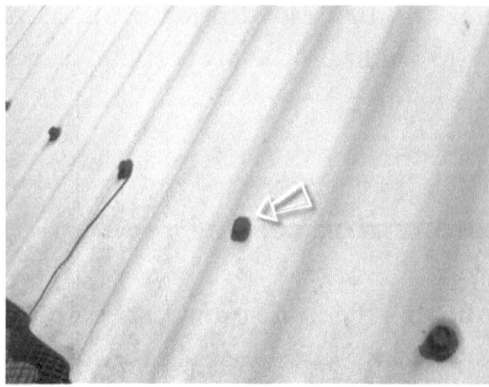

Corrosion of the screw fixings of the corrugated roof coverings.

Roof drainage system

Rainwater goods consist of gutters, which are catchment troughs that are located at the bottom of the roof coverings, which are connected to downpipes. These come in a number of forms and materials, their requirement being to carry the rainwater from the roof to either water storage tanks, or below ground stormwater pipework to council drainage.

Below is an example of what you may find when viewing properties and a guide to some of the maintenance issues you may encounter.

The following depict rainwater goods, gutters, downpipes, water collection and storage tanks, and visual defects you may encounter.

Aluminium rainwater gutters usually employ vertical PVC rainwater pipes and are what we have come to know in modern homes. A visual inspection will usually only show limited defects, especially if you are visiting the property on a dry day, so the things to look for are as follows:

- Water markings on the underside of the gutter and on soffit boarding, which looks like a tide mark. Also, black round marks adjacent the gutter joints caused by water droplets, dripping from the joint. This may indicate a failure of the gutter joints. Take a look at the ground under the gutters around the perimeter of the house. If circumscribed by a concrete path, look for signs of clean area of path caused by wash from an overflowing gutter. The path will appear clean or a lighter colour. If there is a planter bed around the perimeter of the house, are there areas of mulch, soil or grass that has been displaced/washed away?

- Check the joints between gutter and rainwater pipes, also at the junction between the rainwater pipe connections, just above ground level. Admittedly, there may be different types of connections but they all should be adequately connected without damage. Low–level rainwater pipe damage can be caused by impact from lawnmowers or garden whipper snippers etc. All rainwater should be adequately disposed of and not allowed to discharge onto the ground adjacent the property. On occasions, no connection to subterranean drainage is evident, and the pipe discharges water directly onto the ground. This is not generally acceptable, but that being said, you may find this occurring on rural properties. In these situations, it is prudent to seek advice from a licensed builder regarding the requirement for any remedial action, depending on the type and construction of the property and the affects that running water may, or may not have.

- This is an important issue as heavy and constant water discharge adjacent to a property can cause all sorts of structural and maintenance issues. It can also create a conducive environment for termite activity.

- There is also the possibility that inappropriate collection and discharge of rainwater onto the ground may escape onto a neighbour's land, which could create both legal and unforeseen repair costs on the neighbours land!

- Gutters and rainwater pipes should also be adequately secured to the property; there should be no free hanging or loose elements visible.

- Where properties are located in rural locations, with adjacent trees and large shrubs within the yard, it is always prudent to consider the employment of gutter guards.

Below is an example of gutter guards

Many modern houses employ hopper guards over the rainwater gutter and rainwater pipe connections. Care should be taken to ensure these gauze/mesh covers are cleaned regularly, even in areas with no tree foliage to block them. With persistent heavy rain and high humidity, they can quickly become covered with lichen and moss, which makes the rainwater gutters and rainwater pipes ineffective, and even in a moderate downpour, overspill of water can occur.

You can also tell if there is any water overrun over the yard, around or beneath the house, adjacent to the stumps, rutting of the earth can be seen, where the water flow creates ruts or cuts as it flows over the ground.

Water ruts beneath the house, caused by water runoff over the sloping ground. Consideration needs to be given to possible erosion around the pole foundations.

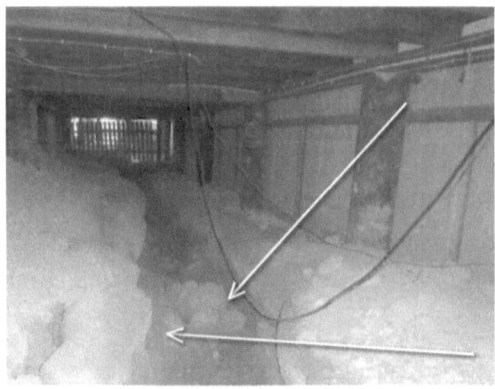

This photograph shows a trench formed beneath a property, to channel rainwater. The sides of the trench have started to collapse, which illustrates there must be significant water flow during storm weather. This is a totally unacceptable control of surface water. The erosion will affect the stability of adjacent stumps, and in turn the integrity of the property.

Asbestos

Associated with older homes, a light to mid-grey looking material, to the untrained eye could be mistaken for cement or concrete. If undamaged and is still adequately allowing the passage of water from the roof, to either storage tank, or below ground drainage, can be left alone. It is, however, recommended that should asbestos be suspected, a full inspection of the property be undertaken, and a report provided, to protect the occupants, visitors to the property, and tradespeople, because of the known risks to health from asbestos products.

A typical sheet asbestos roof. The close lap of the sheeting could be mistaken for a tile roof, which it is not.

Box gutter

This is a hidden gutter that catches water from where two roof lines intersect, or the gutter is hidden by a parapet wall. This is where the external wall projects beyond the gutter line. There are quite a few modern houses with parapet walls, as part of the design, as this type of architecture is currently in vogue. However, this detail is not restricted to modern design, dating back to the building act of 1707 in the city of Westminster, London.

Defects usually consist of poor jointing of the sheet material, atmospheric degradation and corrosion, usually brought about by close proximity to the coast or building debris left within the gutter post–construction. For example, nail, rivet or screw fixings, if left in the gutter, post–construction, and start to corrode, can damage the inner surface and accelerate the ageing process of the gutter.

Box gutters on more modern properties employ an overflow located at the end of the gutter length. The overflow is designed to cater for the possibility of a blockage in the rainwater downpipe. These are usually visible at the end of the gutter run projecting out from the external wall and look like a rectangular box. If the overflow discharges water during rainfall, it is a good indication that the box gutter is blocked. If you visit a property during, or at the end of a dry spell, it is a warning sign that there may be a blockage. If directly beneath the overflow outlet the garden has been washed away or if there is a concrete path or hard standing and the concrete or masonry is cleaner than that around it, this would be a good indication that water falling from the roof has washed away the garden or cleaned the hard standing beneath.

Box gutter at the junction between two dwellings. This detail would normally be out of view from ground level.

It is also important to ensure the gutters are checked regularly for garden debris and children's toys, I have found tennis balls, dolls and cuddly toys lodged within the gutters, leading to a build–up of and inappropriate discharge of water, leading to both internal and external water damage to properties.

This illustration shows corrosion of the roof coverings and gutters blocked with garden debris. This property would benefit from gutter guards and replacement sheet roofing.

Gutter guard in place on this gutter; note that the gutter is free of debris. It is still important to ensure gutter guards are kept clear of debris.

Chimneystacks and solid fuel burning appliances

There are generally two types of chimney stacks, internally or externally constructed, usually from either block, or brickwork and steel exhaust pipes for solid fuel appliances. Defects can arise from water ingress at the junction between the roof coverings and where the stack external face meet. This can be detected via discolouration of the plaster and decorative finishes beneath this point. Water markings and pattern staining will usually be found with mould and mildew growth over the areas concerned.

Corrosion within the external flue/chimney, likely to be a costly fix as this is a two-storey property.

This is a picture of where a steel fire flue passes through the ceiling. Water damage is evident on the plasterboard ceiling; this is a sign the roof is leaking, where the flue passes through the roof coverings.

Chimney stack passing through the roof coverings, the flashing, and the skirt around the base, is a potential weak place, so particular attention should be taken in the roof space and around the base of the stack, where it passes through the roof tiles. This photograph also shows greenery growing from the top of the stack.

Barge boards, fascia boards and soffit boards

These are the boards located at the juncture with the roof, external wall and rainwater goods.

Fascia boarding is the boarding that covers the end of the roof rafters and to which the gutters are secured. Materials used are usually timber or Colorbond, and in older properties may be asbestos.

Soffit boarding is the boarding that covers the underside of the roof rafters between the fascia boarding and the external wall of the house and is horizontal to the ground. Usually boarding such as Hardiflex, a rigid panel sheeting, and in older properties may be asbestos.

Fungal decay within the "V" boarding soffit boarding. This is a more traditional detail. Failure of the gutters has allowed water penetration and decay of the timbers.

Barge boarding and **box end** is the boarding that covers the end final roof rafter above the gable wall of the house, effectively sealing the roof covering between the roof covering and external wall finishes. In older properties the material usually used is timber, but also may be asbestos. Modern homes are more likely to be Colorbond.

The defects you are likely to come across are as follows:

- Timber fascia and barge boards, because they are open to the elements and reliant upon some kind of decorative coating; either varnish or a paint covering. Will require re-application in accordance with the paint manufacturer's recommendations, based upon the location and climate to which they are exposed.

- Most defects such as fungal decay and natural weathering will manifest itself as either discolouration of the timber surface, softening or cuboidal cracking, splits and shakes (the separation of the timber along the grain). The following photograph illustrates decomposition of the timber barge boarding.

Fungal decay within the bargeboard end. Water ingress through the end grain due to failure of the decorative finish has allowed fungal decay to take hold. If on a two or more storey property, consideration should be given to access and additional costs involved in repair/ replacement.

- Although fascia and barge boards are not considered structural, they do provide a fixing point for the rainwater gutters and are instrumental in sealing the roof line at the juncture with the external walls. Therefore, if there is a failure at this point, driving rain may, and usually does, find a way to penetrate into the property, to a greater, or lesser degree.

- The water penetration through poorly-maintained finishes can lead to signs of degradation similar to those described earlier within this guide; loss of paint coverage, uneven surface of the paintwork, paint bubbling, grooves within the decorative finish, in some cases fruiting bodies (this is when the fungus matures and creates spores to propagate).

- Other tell-tale signs are usually found around gutter brackets where the screw fixings have penetrated the paint and timber of the fascia, allowing the passage of moisture. It is quite common for brackets to come loose from the fascia, leading to sagging and deformation of the gutter and thus overspill of water. Any undulation of the gutter is generally quite obvious to the naked eye, visible via sagging of the gutter. Modern properties use aluminium fascia boarding, which is more durable than timber and is therefore less likely to suffer from the above defects.

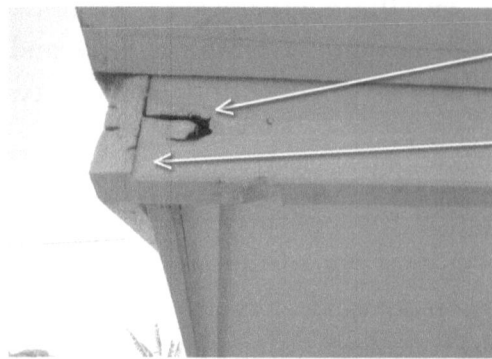

Fungal decay within the fascia and barge board.

Fungal decay within the fascia boarding.

WATER SYSTEMS

If you are viewing a property with a water tank, take the time to establish its condition.

PVC tanks and corrugated steel are today's favourite materials. Pay particular attention to connection points to service pipes. Any leaks will generally manifest as dark staining around and below the pipe connection. It is also important to ensure the mosquito-proof screens that are located at entry and exit pipe connections are regularly cleaned of debris and lichen, which in tropical climates can, in a very short time, lead to blocked inlet and outlet pipes, and in heavy rain, can lead to overspill/inappropriate discharge of water.

Steel tanks have come a long way over the past 20 years, and have good life expectancy, however, older tanks will suffer from corrosion. This is usually visible on the outer side of the tank sheeting and will manifest via brown rust staining. Early stages of corrosion will be visible on the surface finishes, and if you touch the surface, rust will rub off onto your hand. Don't touch heavily rusted steel as you may injure yourself!

It is always better to be proactive and maintain steel tanks. It may be possible to redecorate any early stages of corrosion visible on steel water tanks, however, in some cases, complete renewal should be budgeted for.

In some cases, water tanks are suspended on a timber or steel tank stand; this approach is generally associated with older properties, and certainly rural locations. Care should always be taken not to stand beneath raised tank stands during inspections! There is a considerable amount of weight placed upon the support structure, and therefore, the support frame should be maintained and in a sound structural condition. Any fungal decay, borer or termite activity would compromise a timber structure, leading to a health and safety risk. Steel structures without adequate maintenance and decoration will corrode and succumb to the elements (weather) and can fail the same way a timber support can. It is important to ascertain the condition of the tank and tank stand.

Steel tanks – general considerations when viewing storage tanks are:

- Corrosion on the outer surfaces
- Water markings on the tank emanating from the corroded areas
- Water staining from leaks associated with connections with service pipes

- Water markings on the steel or timber decking supporting the water tank may also give an indication of a failure of the outer wall of the tank
- If you tap the tank, is it holding water or empty? If it's empty directly post a good downpour of rain, this may indicate that it is not fully watertight and requires further investigation. Removal and replacement of the structure will be costly.

Steel water storage tanks, which are in good order, but the timber tank supports have completely succumbed to fungal decay.

Corrosion is visible within the outer finish of this water tank. As the corrosion is working inside out, it is a good indication that this particular tank is at the end of its useful life. The tank is also supported on a timber frame which is directly in contact with the ground and is at risk from fungal decay and termite activity.

For on-ground tank stands, take a look at what the tank is supported on. A concrete slab is ideal for providing support, however, on older properties you may find timber sleepers have been employed. As discussed earlier in this guide, any timber in contact with the ground, even if treated, will eventually succumb to the elements, fungal decay, and the interest of termites to a greater or lesser degree.

Leaking water tanks will also create conducive circumstances for termite activity, as a regular source of water will encourage termite activity, especially if there is a readily available food source close by, for example timber sleeper supports and the like. Remember, once the food source has been expended, and generally before this time, termites will turn their attention to other food sources close by "THE HOUSE!"

Concrete water storage tanks

Generally concrete tanks have a long life expectancy, however, they can suffer from wear and tear, usually in the form of cracks appearing within the outer wall. Once water is able to breach the concrete protection, the steel reinforcement that gives the tank its strength can start to corrode. It is important to pay attention to the external condition of the water tanks whilst viewing the property. A cursory view should give an indication if there are any obvious issues. The illustration below shows a tank which is losing stored water through a crack in the outer wall, and although most cracks if caught early enough can be repaired and made watertight, the longer they are left the more costly the repair. In some instances, depending on the extent of tank degradation, complete replacement may be required. If in doubt, take advice.

The cracks within this water tank wall are very clear to see. There is also water staining on the outer face.

Plumbing pipework visible beneath a high set, pole home or stump supported home

If it is safe to do so, whether you have full upright unhindered access or a visual vantage point from the side of the house, take a look to see if the water pipes look tidy and run in straight lines, and are adequately supported by clips or brackets.

If they are untidy and made up of different materials, for example copper and plastic, this will indicate that alteration or possible previous renovation works have been undertaken. A good tradesman takes pride in his work and will ensure he leaves his work tidy. Evidence of untidy workmanship may be an indication that all is not well with the plumbing of the house.

Water stains on the floorboards beneath the house. Bottom right is the bath waste pipe, which has been leaking. Water pattern staining on the underside of the floor is a good way to locate possible water problems.

If you can, take a look where pipes pass through the floor and walls. Are there any watermarks (pattern staining)? This may indicate a water leak which is not visible within the property. If there is staining, is it wet or damp to touch? If it is, it is likely there is a current leak. The larger wastewater pipes are usually grey (hence the term grey water) and run beneath the house, carrying water from the toilets, kitchen, laundry and bathrooms. A leak from one of these pipes would usually create a rancid smell that you could not mistake — you would smell it first and then by following your nose you would be able to locate the source of the smell, as with water pipes if there is a leak you would see pattern staining and fungal decay evident associated with timbers in close proximity to the leak. Bowing and de-lamination of the floor boarding, if chip boarding, or swelling if craft wood — also referred to as medium density fibreboard, pine or hardwood floor boarding — is less likely to swell quite as much but will still suffer from water marks, softening and will ultimately succumb to fungal decay, it just takes more time to break down, than man-made timber products.

WATER SYSTEMS

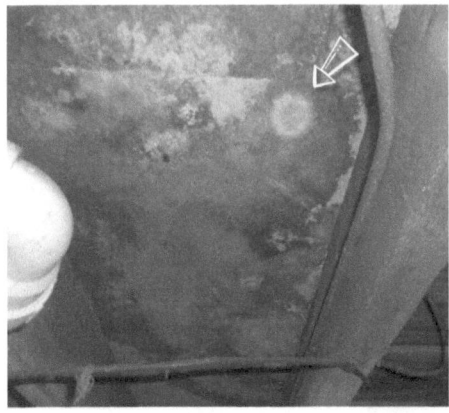

Water pattern staining on the underside of a timber floor caused by a leaking bathroom pipe. The flooring material has begun to deteriorate and lose its strength.

This type of leak beneath a shower area may be costly to rectify.

Water markings (pattern stains) on the underside of the floor boarding indicate a current or past water leak from the plumbing.

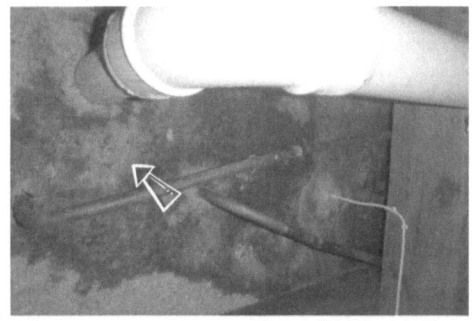

Where pipes pass through the floor, this will generally indicate where the sanitary fittings are above. The location of the damp patch beneath the property will help locate the leaking fitting above. Within the living accommodation, this could be a shower, bath or a wash hand basin, some of which may be accessible, whereas beneath a bath or built-in shower may not. Locating where the water is coming from will give you an idea of the size of the remedial work that may be required. A leaking sink trap or a toilet waste pipe connection which is readily accessible will be less costly than an inaccessible area, which may turn into a much larger job, if once opened up, you found significant timber fungal decay and termite activity!

Supporting timber joists, if in contact with moisture/water leak for a period of time, will suffer from fungal decay. Once again with fungal decay, if not repaired, decayed timbers will attract the unwanted attention of ants and termites. Although ants are only a nuisance, termites have the potential to do significant damage.

Private sewerage treatment plants/septic/bio treatment tanks

Although these are not part of a typical Building and Pest Pre-purchase Inspection, if you are buying a rural property or a property which employs a treatment/septic tank, it would be prudent to obtain any available service documentation through your legal advisor, which is pertinent to the maintenance history of the equipment. In the absence of this, it would be wise to obtain a report from a local treatment plant specialist, on the condition of the unit. The report should include advice on any potential remedial costs involved in bringing it into good repair, should it be required. This is important because should it come to light that there are maintenance issues or the plant is considered defunct due to age, the replacement costs could be significant.

GARDEN AND LANDSCAPING

Walls

Garden walls are generally constructed on a shallow strip foundation and are ideal for stable soil conditions, however, localised poor ground conditions can lead to settlement and movement of the foundations. For example, if trees and large shrubs and bushes are in close proximity of the wall, the root activity can cause damage to the wall, through drying out of the subsoil. Tree trunks that grow close to a garden wall can also cause damage. It would be wise to consider the possible growth of newly–planted and young trees and shrubs that can grow to a substantial size and height, and potentially outgrow their surroundings.

Examples of defects to watch out for are:

- Walls out of vertical alignment, leaning inward or outward
- Cracks in the render coating; these may be vertical, or horizontal
- Stepped cracking within the brickwork walls.

Garden wall dislodged by tree roots.

Fences

Typical 1800mm high close paling garden/yard boundary fence

Timber boundary fences are generally supported by timber posts, concreted into the ground. The fence posts, rails and palings are usually left to weather and turn a silvery colour, although they can stay in service for a considerable time. Because of their dried out state, they can become fragile and susceptible to impact damage.

GARDEN AND LANDSCAPING

It is always important to take note of the condition of both the fence palings, horizontal rails and posts. At first glance, some fences appear to be in a fair condition, but on closer examination, paling bottoms and posts where in contact with the ground can suffer from fungal decay and termite damage.

1000mm to 1200mm picket fence

Picket fence with fungal decay within the lower section of palings. Corrosion of nail fixings is also common, hence loose palings. Always worth a close look.

Decking

Timber decking is a popular way to create inside/outside living and can certainly add to the value and appeal of a property. As with any timber products which are exposed to the elements, the key to longevity is to maintain the timber in accordance with the expected climate and weather conditions, and the correct use of quality decorative preservatives.

To date, hardwood and softwood decking boards are the only practical option. Both are serviceable options, with softwood boarding protected by modern preservatives. Reapplication is key to ensure the serviceability of the timber. Although hardwood has a longer in-service life than softwood, it also requires protection from the elements. This is where most homeowners make the mistake of neglecting the decking, which leads to higher long term expenses and issues with poor inspection results when selling the property.

This large first floor veranda has fungal decay within the supporting joist ends; always a good idea to look up!

New products, for example bamboo-based decking are also now becoming popular, composite products claiming little maintenance costs and long guarantees whilst in service. It would be prudent to look into any composite decking material maintenance requirements, to enable you to maintain it in accordance with the manufacturer's instructions. Therefore, requesting any maintenance information from the vendor is key. Google is a good reference point to locate technical information on products.

Decking tends to decay quicker on the underside, and in many cases appears to be in a sound condition on the upper wearing side. This is due to the inaccessibility of the underside, making it difficult or not possible to maintain with preservative. High humidity in tropical areas also add to the start of fungal decay.

When walking on the decking, use the heel test – stand on your toes and rock back onto your heels, dropping your full body weight down. The deck should feel solid with no deflection underfoot. If you feel springing, this may indicate fungal decay or other damage.

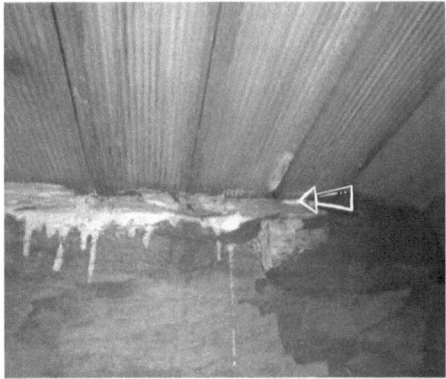

Fungal timber decay within the timber supporting joist of an external raised deck.

Main supporting joist beneath a timber deck with evidence of fungal decay. The joist is soft on the surface and has started to lose its structural integrity. The white fungus on the surface is a visual key indicator that there are issues with structural integrity and further investigation is required by a Building Contractor.

Mechanical fixings used to secure the decking to the supporting framework are either screw or nail fixings. Screws are the better choice as they don't generally allow the decking to twist and work loose underfoot. Nails tend to work their way loose and create a trip hazard. Nails, therefore, require annual maintenance with regards to checking and resecuring them. Screw fixings are more costly and therefore not used as often as nails.

If you can't see for yourself, request confirmation from your building inspector to check if the decking support posts are either timber directly secured into the ground, or the timber posts are connected to steel stirrups, as any timber in contact with the ground will eventually decay. You will then be aware that maintenance is likely to be required sooner rather than later if timber ground contact is evident.

Timber deck support leg in direct contact with the earth/ground.

GARDEN AND LANDSCAPING

This photograph shows the correct use of steel supports to the base of the timber posts to ensure they are not in contact with the ground.

As with paths and planter beds, the decking should finish a minimum of 75mm beneath the weep holes and termite management system. If not, there should be a space of not less than 25mm between the edge of the decking and the external face of the wall of the property. This creates a visual inspection zone. You could also incorporate a removable section of deck to allow the concealed area to be inspected.

The configuration of this deck means that the external brick wall weep holes are out of sight, lying beneath the decking.

There should be at least a 25mm gap between the decking and face of the eternal wall or have a removable strip of decking along the length of the juncture between deck and wall, to allow removal for a visual inspection.

One of the mistakes made when building a deck or outside entertaining area of a property is to include cabinetry fitted against the external wall of the property covering the termite management system, render striker joint and weep holes. It is important to ensure the termite management system guarantees are not compromised or made invalid because of obstructions. If the property is within the guarantee period, also check if the vendors have kept up with annual inspections.

If the block is a sloping site with a raised deck with steps leading from it, take a look at the condition of the steps (if they are timber). Check what they are sat upon. The strings (the side runners of the steps) and bottom riser should be sat/supported by a concrete slab or paving and not directly onto the ground, as direct contact with the earth will allow fungal decay and termite interest. If not supported properly, the steps may sink into the ground and become unsafe to use.

This external stairway/steps is supported on a concrete step; there is, therefore, no direct contact with the earth/ground. However, the timber has not been adequately maintained with preservative and is suffering from weathering and fungal decay.

It is always prudent to look closely at veranda timbers, as they are exposed to the elements, and if extensive, for example, Queenslander properties of some age, will be costly to maintain, especially if they have been neglected. Nail fixings may have corroded out.

Timber handrails and balustrades generally decay at joints and junction points, also where standing rainwater can occur. Poor decorative condition will also accelerate the rate of fungal decomposition. You should also take into consideration that once decay has taken hold, the structural integrity of the element will, without repair, eventually come into question.

Handrail/balustrade with fungal decay and not fit for purpose, (risk of fall).

Stepped access to properties can also cause issues if the distance from the access path to the door threshold is more than 570mm in height., If this is the case, a landing is required to alight, walk onto, prior to exiting the property to avoid trips and falls.

Any landing over 1000mm in height also requires a handrail around its edge and down the slope of the steps.

A general point of note with respect to a property which has been recently decorated, prior to being placed for sale on the open market. It is quite easy to conceal fungal decay behind recent decorating works, and one should be vigilant when examining the external finishes. Your inspector will be fully aware of what to look for; the tell-tale signs, which have been discussed thus far.

For pole houses and properties supported by timber, steel or concrete stumps, it is not uncommon for the property owners to employ some kind of timber trellis or fencing material to partially enclose the underside of the house, in an attempt to make it more aesthetically pleasing. In doing this, many make the mistake of placing the timber material directly in contact with the ground but doing so will lead to fungal decay. It also creates a bridge for access of crawling pests such as ants, and of course is an attractive environment for termite activity, and a possible access point to the property.

Always pay attention to trellis. Because the timber sections are small, they succumb to fungal decay quite early if not maintained, or as with this example, in contact with the ground is a food source for termites.

Pay particular attention to the detailed fretwork such as softwood brackets, which in most cases, don't offer any structural use, but are decorative only. Fungal decay can take hold if the external decorations are not maintained.

Planter beds

Garden planter beds are usually constructed from either softwood or hardwood timber frames, consisting of vertical support posts and horizontal sleepers. It's also not uncommon to find concrete pavers and concrete edges. The use of timber in preference to concrete is mainly based upon cost; it's generally cheaper to use timber.

Even if treated with preservatives, because of its contact with the ground, timber will eventually succumb to fungal decay. Timber mulch is also a favourite within garden beds. Care should be taken in these circumstances as both timber frames, edging and mulch are a magnet for termites.

It is quite common for house yards to have planter beds, many are constructed up against the external wall of the property. You should pay particular attention to the height of the planter bed, where timber and brick veneer walls are employed and look for signs that the planter is not obscuring the weep holes, and in turn compromising the termite management system of the property.

A planter bed abutting an external wall obscuring the weep holes at the base of the wall.

Timber retaining walls

Timber retaining walls are a popular and affordable method of landscaping. They offer quick and easy methods of sculpting your yard. Treated timbers will provide longevity to the in-service life of the material. The things to look for whilst viewing the property are as follows:

- Look for soft spongy areas, holes and areas of missing timber within the sleepers and the supporting posts
- Cuboidal cracking and disintegration of the timber
- The timber is loose, dry and dust-like with hollow tunnels visible
- It is quite usual for the supporting vertical posts to suffer from fungal decay from water penetration through the top face of the post
- Retaining walls may appear in a sound condition but on closer inspection at the base of the support posts (just below ground level) is where the decay is taking place, compromising the integrity of the retaining wall.

Fungal decay within the post bottom and adjacent horizontal of sleeper of the retaining wall. It is always prudent to take a look at all the timber garden walls for any evidence of decay.

Fungal decay within the post bottom and adjacent horizontal sleeper of the retaining wall.

Where the walls are quite high and there is a risk of a build-up of surface water from the earth beyond (which may be from a neighbour's garden) pay particular attention for signs of running water. This will usually manifest in the following tell-tale signs:

- Water marking on the timber wall
- Earth washed away from the base of the wall. Settlement of the ground level to the rear of the retainer may indicate soil and small particles are being washed through the joints of the sleepers.

Timber retaining wall which has collapsed due to termite activity and fungal decay. When tapped, the top sleeper looks and sounds to be in good order, but in actual fact, is in poor condition with over 50% of the unseen side eaten out by decay and termites.

Paths and driveways

Concrete is the favoured method for paths and driveways within a residential yard area as it is very hard wearing, and if laid correctly will create a safe, even surface. Brick cobbles – or sets as they are also known – create effective driveways and paths, and also make access to the ground beneath for maintenance, should it be required, a lot easier than having to break up an existing hard standing.

GARDEN AND LANDSCAPING

It is important to lay the concrete path around the perimeter of the property with a slight cross fall to ensure rainwater runs away from the external wall and not towards it. It is also important that there are no low areas where standing water can pool.

Look out for cracks in the path where settlement has taken place, leading to a trip hazard. Pay attention to the adjacent yard finishes; does it look like the land is running downward towards the path? This may indicate that there may be standing water and a possible drainage problem of rainwater during inclement weather

Look at the junction with the path and external wall of the house. If there is a sizeable gap, it may indicate the path is parting company with the wall, settlement of the path. It is not uncommon for a little movement to be experienced in some instances, however, if the path is perched on top of a bank or adjacent to a retaining wall with a drop beyond, movement of the path may be a sign something is going on!

Depression within the brick driveway, with trip hazards and standing water to consider.

Trip hazard, settlement of the brick paving.

Uneven brick paving, trip hazards; repair will be quite time consuming. Consideration should be given to this, and the overall area of brick paving that requires attention.

The crack running to the left of the rainwater pipe is a thermal expansion joint and supposed to be there and still considered serviceable.

Trees and shrubs

Trees and shrubs play an important role in landscaping and the overall appeal of a property, therefore their planning and location within a yard should be considered carefully. Many Australian species, if in the right location, will have quite extraordinary growth, and can quickly outgrow where they have been placed, while smaller plants in the wrong location can cause just as much havoc.

Large palm tree close to the roof of a property. Consideration should be given to falling fronds and the suitability of the close proximity of the tree to the property.

The root system of grass, trees and shrubs are a natural method of ground stabilisation. The removal of and significant pruning of plant life should not be undertaken without specialist arborist advice first. Excessive pruning of trees can lead to stress growth. This is where the tree will put significant effort into regaining its crown size, as trees actually process the minerals which are extracted from the ground, by their roof system, in their leaves, through photosynthesis. The tree would therefore effectively die without enough leaves, within the crown, to allow it to process minerals taken from the soil.

If we consider the close proximity of trees and mature bushes to a home, we have to look at two possible problems that can arise from this:

- Tree and bush branches can harbour pests and create a bridge into the property, where branches come into contact with roofs, gutters and external walls. This makes it easier for crawling bugs such as ants to get into the roof space. Also, vermin rats, mice and possums will take advantage of the bridge your landscaping has created.

- Bushes and scrubs at low level around the perimeter of a property (within planter beds) if left to their own devices can obscure the external walls and hide evidence of termite activity.

- Mature trees within your neighbour's yard with large limbs that over-sail the boundary of the property is known as an encroachment.

Consideration should be given to the health of the tree and if any remedial action is required to ensure it remains safe and healthy. Some trees will have protection orders attached to them by Council.

Advice from a reputable licensed gardening/arborist company and licensed pest control contractor is recommended at either the onset or before taking up occupation, to be aware of any potential maintenance costs.

PART 3
INTERNAL

WALLS

Internal walls and internal face of external walls in modern properties are generally softwood timber partition, but can in some cases be steel frame, with a gyprock/plasterboard covering.

The timber framework of the walls may be a number of different types of species of softwood. Older properties or speculatively constructed houses may have hardwood timber frames, as hardwood is less likely to succumb to termite attack. Hardwood is also more resistant to fungal decay, but not immune. Another option for wall framing which is increasingly becoming popular is steel, which has benefits of being lightweight, strong and not at risk from fungal decay and termite damage.

FINISHES - INTERNAL WALL AND CEILINGS

Gyprock (plasterboard) is widely used for internal partitions of both commercial and residential dwellings. It is made from Gypsum, which is a naturally-occurring non-toxic sedimentary rock which when sandwiched between a paper liner, this creates a lightweight sheeting product, which is favoured by the building industry. Along with plaster or polystyrene ceiling covings, the Gyprock boards are secured via either nail or screw fixings, when secured to timber or steel stud walls.

Polystyrene tiles were used in the past because of their textured finish and insulation value.

They are flammable and a fire risk.

The favoured method is via either nail or screw fixings. Where Gyprock is secured to brick or blockwork walls, dabs of Gyprock adhesive are used to glue the boards direct to the wall or to timber battens.

If kept in a dry environment and not mistreated, the sheet product will have a reasonably long working lifespan. However, should it be exposed to a constant supply of water through a leaking pipe, external wall or roof covering, it will quite quickly start to deteriorate, fall apart and become soft and clay–like.

Tell–tale signs of water decomposition of Gyprock is usually one or a combination of the following:

- A musty smell, and mould staining on the decorative surface
- Sagging of ceiling boards
- Boarding which is in a serviceable condition when tapped with your knuckle or a screwdriver will give off a high pitched sound; boarding which is in a poor condition will have a dull thud
- Damp or water–damaged boarding will also swell as it absorbs moisture and will be uneven when you run your hand upon it. This will be more noticeable at board joints and edges. You can also use a torch to shine along the surface of the boarding to detect uneven surfaces. Shining the torch along the surface at 90 degrees to the surface rather than shining it directly at the wall is a handy trick to show up defects.

Other places to look are around window and door openings, and at the juncture between the wall and ceiling boards.

FINISHES - INTERNAL WALL AND CEILINGS

Solid masonry walls are generally used within unit blocks, where concrete blocks are employed for both the internal face of external walls and internal partition walls. In earlier buildings, the blockwork may be exposed and just painted, or a render or solid plaster coating applied to the surface of the blockwork.

It is not uncommon for condensation to be a problem in older unit blocks constructed from concrete blockwork or solid brickwork, because of the mass of the building materials. They take a significant amount of time to heat up, unlike lightweight materials. Therefore, when there is a period of continued high humidity and the walls are cool to touch, moisture which is suspended/held in the warm air will condensate back to a liquid state on the cold wall surface. This can create favourable conditions for mould growth. A neat trick to ascertain if there is mould growth is, as discussed earlier, is to shine your torch at 90 degrees to the wall surface. If there is any mould present, it will show up as a layer of white furry material on the surface of the wall.

Older residential dwellings may have asbestos sheeting instead of Gyprock. Used as internal wall and ceiling boarding, asbestos was made illegal as a product and could not be used or reused in any shape or form from 2003 throughout Australia. This is where your inspector would be able to advise on further specialist investigations.

Asbestos sheeting has a smooth finish room facing and has a dimpled back surface. Sheets are smaller in size to its Gyprock counterpart and therefore can generally be identified. There is a high likelihood for older properties to have asbestos because the board joints are covered with a timber cover strip, usually in the region of 30–50mm wide and 12mm thick. If in good condition with no damage and sealed with a decorative finish, asbestos can remain in service, however, if it becomes damaged and there are open ends where fibres can become airborne, there is a potential for significant risk to health.

Because asbestos is poor at resisting impact damage, it is quite common for older properties to have damaged boarding, with the occupants oblivious to the risk it poses. It is also not uncommon for cracked and damaged asbestos boards to have masking tape or other equal, tape repair over the cracks. If in doubt, and if you know the estimated age of the property, assume there is likely to be asbestos present. The property inspector will indicate if they think asbestos is present but will not undertake any tests on your behalf. A special instruction is required for an appropriately qualified inspector (this can be the inspector you have engaged if appropriately qualified/licenced) to carry out an asbestos audit.

It is not uncommon to find timber weatherboarding on internal walls, certainly if alterations have taken place, where the external terrace or veranda has been enclosed to form internal living space. This may be an early sign of alterations being carried out to the property. A question posed to the inspector may be prudent in this case.

FLOORS

Floor finishes can be solid concrete, usually associated with modern building ground floors which either have a ceramic tile carpet or laminated timber covering. In some instances, the concrete floor may be exposed and polished to create an acceptable finish. Some floors, where visible, for example in the garage, may be cracked, usually 1mm or less in width. This can be caused by high temperatures and winds that dry out the concrete a little too fast once it has been poured. These cracks are usually just within the upper surface of the concrete slab. Should you notice larger, more substantial cracks, say for example within the garage where the concrete is readily visible, further investigation would be in order.

Hogging or sagging of a concrete floor where it feels like you are either walking up or down hill may be due to settlement of the substrata ground beneath, leading to subsequent settlement of the concrete slab or a chemical reaction taking place which has led to the concrete expanding, leading to what is known as hogging. Should a suspended concrete slab be employed with the above defects noted, this may indicate that one or a number of the concrete support columns or piles have suffered from subsidence (settlement). A manifestation of these defects, if in evidence, would require the services of a structural engineer for further examination and determination of the possible cause and financial implications in rectification if deemed necessary.

FANS AND AIR CONDITIONING

Ceiling fans

Although these don't form part of the pre-purchase inspection, it is prudent to take the time to check a couple of the ceiling fans for operation. It is a common failure for the three-speed fans to develop a fault, where it only works on one speed. This is usually a fault with the capacitor, which is the more commonly used method of speed control. There may therefore be costs for repair you are not aware of.

Take a look at the fan blade edges. In humid climates the humidity, and if close to the beach, salt air, will speed up decomposition of the paint finish, leading to corrosion.

Air conditioning and condensate pipes

Condensate pipes should be connected to drainage in an approved manner (assuming the drainage is not connected to any water harvesting device) or at least discharge away from the house. Pay particular attention to where the pipe discharges, any water source depositing on the ground near a property will create conditions conducive for termite foraging and activity. During prolonged dry periods if the condensate pipe is running, this will create a ready and valuable supply of moisture for termites.

This is a condensate pipe running from the A/C unit. It should either discharge away from the external wall of the house or into drainage. In its current state it creates conducive conditions for termite activity. When looking around the perimeter of the house, pay particular attention to open pipework near the A/C unit.

DOORS

Internal doors in modern homes are usually lightweight construction with a plywood or craft wood veneer, some of which are steam pressed to create the effect of raised and fielded panels or grooves for artistic and decorative effect. If treated with care they will generally last a long time, however, if subjected to impact damage or heavy usage, will lead to early wear and tear and loss of functionality. When dealing with low quality, speculatively constructed houses generally aimed at the rental market or first time market entrants, the quality of the finishing is likely to be quite low. Pay particular attention to the condition of door ironmongery, door latches and handles for the bathroom and check that toilet door locks work properly. Take note if the handles are in the horizontal position when not in use, and not sloping downward, which would indicate the latches and handles are worn and towards the end of their useful life. There is little or no adjustment built into the cheaper door ironmongery. If the handles are loose it may be possible to tighten them up, as some handle types have a cover over the screw fixings, which with the aid of a screwdriver, may pop off to reveal hidden fixings. If there are a number of worn door sets it may prove difficult to purchase matching replacement sets, as suppliers move with current architectural trends. This scenario would leave you in the unfortunate position of odd door sets throughout the house.

Door handle loose. The outer cover can be removed in most cases, to reveal fixing screws.

Cast your eye along the bottom edge of the internal doors, especially where tile floors are employed. Constant mopping of floors along the door bottom can lead to swelling and de-lamination of the door. Depending on the outer sheet material, this can be detected via the outer bottom edge of the door being uneven, flaking or becoming furry, almost fibrous, once a door has succumbed to de-lamination or degradation of the bottom edge through water damage. There is no satisfactory repair option; the only practical option is to replace the door. This, as with ironmongery, poses the problem that if the doors are a number of years old and a discontinued line, you may have to put up with a non-matching door in the house, which will stand out if in an obvious place next to original doors.

DOORS

Delamination of the door bottom. Water damage - this looks like bubbling of the outer veneer and loss of paint coverage. A replacement door would be in order here.

INTERNAL TIMBERWORK

Architraves and skirting boards

Architraves and skirting boards are usually softwood timber, although craft wood is also used (Medium Density Fibre boarding [MDF] or craft wood as it is commonly known in Australia). This material is usually good in service as long as it doesn't come into contact with persistent regular water, through for example, mopping tiled floors or used within bathrooms or kitchens, where constant water penetration is possible. Where craft wood is in constant contact with water, it will swell and start to become fibrous, and lose its decorative/paint covering. Once this has started to occur, there is nothing that can be done, other than replacement of the affected length of material. These skirting boards and architraves are not structural and are employed to cover joints or junction points, where the floor meets the wall, and where the doorframe meets the wall boarding.

This length of architrave is located directly above the kitchen sink. Constant water splashes have led to the deterioration and integrity of the material.

Softwood timber is a prime target for termite attack, should the termite management system (barrier) of the property be breached. Once inside the home termites will search out palatable timber and consume it. They are private creatures that go about their business with stealth, leaving the paint covering behind, only consuming the timber. Termite activity usually only becomes apparent when mechanical impact occurs, where the outer surface is damaged/breached. Termites will consume timber from the entry point to the building and work both upward and outward along the walls and floor timbers. When termites consume the inner timber of a tree, the only way is up and down within the trunk, whereas with a house they get distracted and disorientated and so head along joists and framework, both vertically and horizontally, including window reveals and window boarding.

Termite damage leaves hollow groove–like workings along the length of the timber. It is very important that if active termites are found within a property that they are not disturbed, as they will retreat from the place of activity if they perceive a threat. It is advised that specialist advice be sought from a licensed pest technician regarding suitable treatment, to eradicate the queen and nest. It is significantly more difficult to treat termites when

INTERNAL TIMBERWORK

you can't properly access them. There is usually a musty smell associated with rotting timber, especially where it is not always visible because it is encapsulated, for example beneath a shower tray or to the rear of a tile splashback of a shower, laundry area, or under a bath. A musty smell is a good indicator that all is not well and there is likely to be some kind of timber decay or pest attack taking place.

Termites have destroyed the integrity of this timber floor joist, adjacent to a staircase. The joist is completely hollow with loss of its entire load bearing capability.

You should look out for uneven or broken paintwork where the timber is either spongy or dry, with breakable sections of timber, which is missing. This is classic fungal decay.

Structural movement due to fungal decay, timber borer or termite damage within a timber framed off ground pole or stump house.

The tell-tale signs that are usually evident within this type of property will be as follows:

- Walking up or down hill within the property – humps in the floor where as you walk through the property you feel like you walk into the floor or stub your toe; also, the floor isn't where you naturally anticipate it should be. This is usually a sign of either the supporting stumps have settled into the ground or are suffering from fungal decay or termite damage, and have therefore lost their structural integrity, effectively now being compressed by the imposed load of the house.

- Another possible factor is that the house has been restumped and adequate temporary support has not been implemented, which has facilitated uneven settlement of the house as work progressed.

- Other tell–tale signs of this type of uneven settlement can also manifest in other defects throughout the property. As the building twists and becomes out of level alignment, door and window frames are vulnerable, leading to frames becoming out of alignment, with doors not opening, closing or latching correctly, and sitting poorly in their twisted frames.

- Doors may catch on the frame heads and also floor finishes. Windows are usually difficult to operate; both sliding and traditional hinged opening windows may be difficult to open and close.

- If the settlement is quite severe, kitchen, bathroom cupboards and benchtops can become out of level. Shower cubicle doors can also be affected, which can lead to water escaping from the shower enclosure, which in turn can lead to fungal decay of surrounding finishes, and water is of course conducive for termite activity.

INTERNAL TIMBERWORK

- What needs to be established at this point; is this an ongoing problem or has the movement been arrested/stopped, and what documentary evidence is there to support/confirm this? If there is no evidence of a paperwork trail regarding historical remedial works, then you will require the services of a structural engineer or licensed builder to examine the property and offer written advice as to any required remedial action. Sometimes structural settlement requires a period of monitoring – over a full 12-month season – to establish if the movement is progressive or has arrested post remedial works.

- Other reasons for uneven floors within a raised property may be attributed to current or historical borer damage. The more severe the damage to the timber, the more severe the structural movement may seem. Borers like sapwood and generally head for softwood floor boarding and adjacent softwood timber framing.

- Beetle damage of timber in service in Queensland is usually attributed to Anobium Punctatum (furniture beetle) and will generally attack pine timber, which has generally been in service for in excess of 20 years. They are also known to attack spotted gum and English oak.

The inspector will determine if further investigation or possible treatment is required. There is no guarantee post treatment that a further outbreak will not commence. This is due to the lifecycle of the beetle, as they only emerge from the timber at the time they are fully mature and looking for a mate, therefore they can spend up to three years boring backwards and forwards in the timber without being discovered. They exit the timber by creating exit/flight holes. These are usually beneath the floor on the underside and therefore not always seen/discovered unless you have access to inspect.

Floor coverings such as carpets, vinyl, timber veneers and tile coverings also hide evidence of any activity on the upper side of the floor finishes. Damage to timbers are usually heaviest in damper locations of a house, therefore leading to more extensive damage to cellars and timbers where the moisture content is higher, for example, bathrooms, toilets and outbuildings. The evidence of frass, a light coloured dust around the exit/flight holes within the surface of the timber, and if the holes are light coloured, may be an indication of recent beetle activity.

The absence of frass, and if the flight holes are darker in appearance, may be an indication of old activity.

Calymmaderus incisus (Queensland pine beetle) likes hoop pine sapwood, which is found in structures such as floors and walls of older homes, and rarely found in roof timbers. If untreated, it will reinfest until the timber is fully destroyed.

Modern building codes and building methods has decreased the risk of attack to timbers in service, and reports of current damage have become less frequently noted but do still occur. Evidence of activity is usually within older properties, some of which may have been relocated from their original site of construction. This is more prevalent in traditional Queenslander homes that have been renovated on a new site.

INTERNAL TIMBERWORK

Cabinetry

Although the rule of thumb is to measure the property you are inspecting in comparison with other type and age dwellings, I will point out the tell-tale signs of wear and tear, amongst other things, to allow you to view the finishings objectively.

Look at the cabinetry as a whole. Is it in good order? Is it modern and in keeping with current trends? You may be looking at a home for possible renovation and the cabinetry is not a big deal as you have budgeted for an upgrade? Let's just look at that proposal for a second. In some cases, if the cabinetry is in good order but dated, you may wish to consider remodelling rather than complete replacement. To make this decision you will need to evaluate the current condition of the cabinetry. So, let's look at some easy steps to making that decision.

These checks are also pertinent to evaluating modern cabinetry.

Check the door hinges by opening and closing the doors. Do the doors open and close freely or do they catch on adjacent doors or drawers?

Check the edging of the doors, drawers and carcass. Are there any loose sections along which you can see or flick with your fingernail?

Is the carcass free from chemical or water stains which have led to swelling or deterioration of the finishes?

What condition are the kicker plates (these are located at the bottom front, where the carcass meets the floor)? And where visible, check the cupboard sides — look for swelling of the bottom edge. This is a sign of water damage, usually attributed to mopping and cleaning of floors. Not all bottom edges of the kicker plates or cabinetry are sealed and are at risk from water damage over time, more so with wet floor areas.

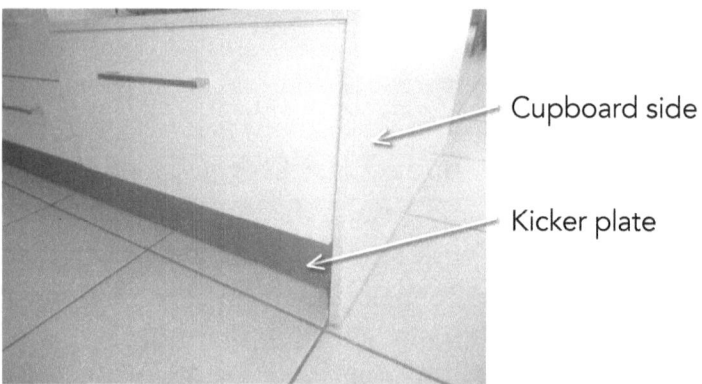

Water damage is usually noted by swelling of the board material, thus the edging strips are not wide enough to cover the board edge. Once this has taken place, decomposition accelerates as water absorption increases.

Laminated benchtops within the kitchen are usually roll edge finish, whereas benchtops within the bathrooms, en-suite and laundry are generally square edge. Take your time and look for de-lamination; this is where the laminated covering of the benchtop begins to lose its adhesive fix with the plywood beneath, usually detected by tapping the laminate top. It will feel like it has started to bubble and will allow you to push it up and down. Check also that there are no undulations abutting the wash hand basin, kitchen sink or laundry bowl. This defect may indicate water damage and unseen fungal decay within the plywood or chipboard beneath.

Stone benchtops come in various thicknesses and qualities. Cracks and impact damage are usually very easy to spot, so just take a little time to cast your eye around the surfaces and edges.

This is a good reminder that having your trusty torch with you allows you to shine the torch at 90 degrees, either to benchtop or flat surface finish of the cabinet, to look for undulation and imperfections in the sheet material. If you're looking at a flat surface now, give it a go! It's quite surprising what it will show up to you.

Wear and tear of cabinetry will depend on three main factors:

- Quality – cost of manufacture
- How much use will they receive?
- Have they been mistreated?

The action/movement of drawers is always a bone of contention. If the cabinets are of low quality, they will age quickly. There are some good examples of European ironmongery used in modern Australian cabinetry; soft close doors and drawers, push action, opening doors etc. You will know when you test the operation of the doors and drawers whether they are of good quality or not. Older cabinetry will more than likely be poor in operation and fitting, and it will be obvious straight away. You should take this into consideration when deciding on possible future expenditure.

Some modern home designs suspend the basin and bathroom cabinetry off the wall, creating a clear void beneath. This is especially popular in wet rooms, as the cabinets don't come into contact with water deposited on the floor.

Floor and wall tiling

Defects associated with both wall and floor tiling in wet areas are generally associated with either a failure of the grouting or cracks within the tiles, due to age and wear and tear. Both these defects allow the passage/ migration of moisture to the rear of the tile, and subsequent decomposition of the finishes beyond, leading to a loss of key/adhesion of the tiles. If you tap the tile front there is a good chance you will hear a hollow sound (drumming). Tiles on unaffected walls or floor will have a high pitch sound when tapped but loose tiles will have a low audible pitch.

If moisture has beached the tiles and the property is of some age, before modern waterproof barriers were used, there is likely to be fungal decay of the finishes beyond.

The shower water has breached the tiles and waterproofing, leading to deterioration of the floor finishes beyond, hence the cracked tile and spring in the floor finishes.

INTERNAL TIMBERWORK

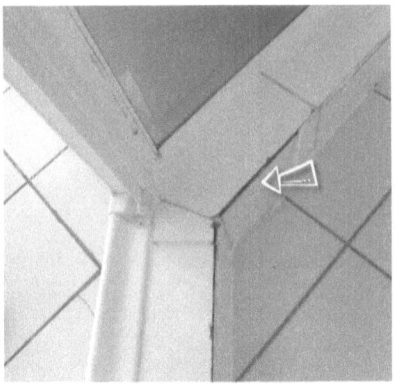

The grout along the tile edge has deteriorated with age and has been substituted with silicone sealant, which has failed, allowing the passage of water, hence the failure of the adjacent floor tiles (refer to previous photograph).

INTERNAL PLUMBING

Hot and cold water pipes beneath wash hand basins and within laundry and kitchen cupboards are generally easily accessible. You can easily run your fingers over the joints of the pipework where they connect and check for leaks. You have to be careful in hot, humid areas that you don't mistake condensation forming on a cold water pipe for a leak. A leak will be visible because water will run from a joint or connection in the pipe. It will run along the pipe then drip off at the bend or junction. Condensation will generally look like there are water droplets the full length of the surface of pipe. If you suspect a leak, use a tissue or cloth to wipe the joint dry. Wait a few seconds and water will appear again and run from the offending joint. Condensation, however, will take longer for the build-up of moisture along the length of the pipe.

Water stain on the ceiling boarding. Further investigation is required here to establish if it is current or historical.

Water stain on the ceiling boarding. Further investigation is required here to establish if it is current or historical.

Leaking waste pipes will also produce a smell. The usual suspect will be the connections around the trap under the sink or basin. These types of leaks are commonplace, due to the fact that the trap requires cleaning out from time to time. You can undertake a simple test to establish if the trap has become blocked with debris such as hair etc. Turn on the tap and fill the basin with 50mm of water — more if you require — and then time to see how long it takes for the sink/basin to drain the water. If it takes quite a long time and bubbles flow up from the plughole, then the trap requires attention. This task is easy to do and can be done in about 15–20 minutes.

INTERNAL PLUMBING

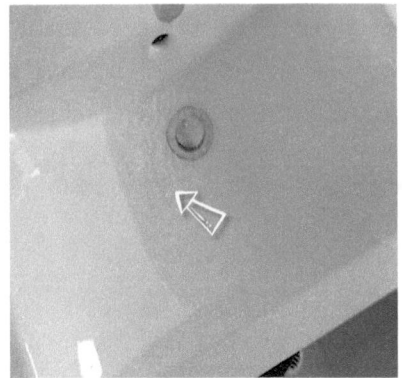

Vanity basin with slow running wastewater because the trap beneath the basin is blocked.

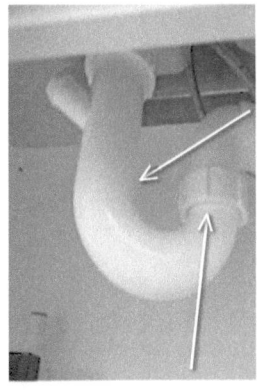

Waste trap beneath the vanity basin debris. Build-up in the trap, leading to slow water flow from the basin. This is quite easy to remove and clean out, albeit an unpleasant task!

Whilst viewing the sanitary appliances, turn the taps on and off quite quickly. If there is a banging sound as you turn off the water flow, this is what is called water hammer and usually occurs when the pipework within the timber wall frame has either popped out of its clip fixing or has never been clipped properly. It can also be a factor of high water pressure. This banging of the pipes has become more audible with modern taps. The constant banging caused by the water hammer can in some cases lead to damage to pipe joints and subsequent leaks occurring. It is annoying to hear the water hammer when either the washing machine or dishwasher calls for water during its washing cycle. There are proprietary methods to resecure the loose pipes and install shock absorbers that can be employed to reduce the effect of water hammer. Your local plumber can assist with this problem.

TERMITE DAMAGE

This section looks at a few examples of termite damage within timbers in use at a residential property, illustrating what can and does show up in an pre purchase building and timber pest inspection.

The word termite sends most homeowners and prospective purchasers into a blind panic, and with some good reason. Termites are responsible for significant economic loss to property throughout Australia. We should acknowledge that, we humans have encroached into termite territory, cutting down their natural habitat and removing their readily available food source.

A termite colony sees our homes as square trees and a possible place to find a food source and shelter.

Not all nests are above or on the ground, or even within trees. It is not always possible to detect their activity by merely walking through a property. So let's look at what the inspector might find during his inspection.

Termite shelter tubes (mudding) visible on the underside of the termite capping of a traditional timber stump beneath a property. The capping has done its job in forcing out the termites into clear view. The stump, however, along with other stumps of this property, are completely eaten out, compromising the structural integrity of the building.

The inspector will attempt to locate the Durable Notice – this indicates what, if any, termite management is in place. The first point of call is the electric meter and fuse cupboard, usually located on the outside of the property. The other possible location is on the inner side of the kitchen sink cabinetry.

A typical durable notice will give the name and details of the installation contractor and will indicate how the property is protected regarding termite management, for example, perimeter of the building, penetrations, and piers/columns etc. In the absence of a durable notice, the inspector would have to assume there is no protection offered to the property. There may be more than one durable notice if the property is of some age, so it is therefore important the inspector takes note of the dates on the notice, along with the method of protection.

It is not uncommon for protection to have expired as not all owners chose to maintain the termite management of their property. Either way, the inspector would then be able to offer advice as to the correct course of action concerning continuation or the requirement for installation of a termite management system.

Examples of termite damage within a dwelling:

Termite damage within the window reveal. The timber has been eaten out. The damage to the decorative finish was due to investigation works by an inspector.

Termite damage within an internal doorframe. This was an easy one to spot as gaffer tape had been used to cover the damage to the doorframe.

Top plate of the wall within the roof space, eaten out by termites. They also caused significant damage to the adjacent roof trusses.

Cyclone rod affected by the timber damage, now loose.

The top section of the timber roof truss has been completely destroyed. Also visible is the earthen tunnels (mudding) created by the foraging termites to allow them to go about their business protected.

This is a pile of stored softwood beneath a property. The termites are well established. This is why you should not store timber beneath a dwelling in direct contact with the ground!

TERMITE DAMAGE

The termite nest in this roof space photograph is made out of hardwood pulp which has come from the structure of the property!

This photograph shows mudding on the surface of roof timbers. Remember, to get to this location, the termites have passed edible timber in the lower structure.

WHERE TO NEXT?

I hope this book has changed the way you look at a potential new home. It isn't my intention to dissuade you from making a purchase, but the contrary; I want you to put down your roots, but to have an understanding of what you are buying. There is and never will be a fault—free home. I'm sure when you attend your next open home, post reading this book, you will look at the property as a group of components working together as one. Yes, you will see the potential new home, but it will be broken down into elements, some of which will have failures and maintenance issues, which hopefully you will see, be more aware and ultimately question during your decision—making process of whether to put in that all—important offer.

At that point, should you wish to proceed further, you will be better placed to discuss the home with your chosen licensed building and pest inspector.

HAPPY HUNTING!

Contact details
www.propertyinspectionssunshinecoast.com.au
info@propertyinspectionssunshinecoast.com.au

NOTES

NOTES

www.ingramcontent.com/pod-product-compliance
Lightning Source LLC
Chambersburg PA
CBHW021154080526
44588CB00008B/329